INCREDIBLE BUGS

Thanks to the creative team:
Senior Editor: Alice Peebles
Fact checking: Kate Mitchell
Design: www.collaborate.agency

Hungry Tomato™
A division of Lerner Publishing Group, Inc.
241 First Avenue North
Minneapolis, MN 55401 USA

For reading levels and more information,
look up this title at www.lernerbooks.com.

Main body text set in Mate Regular 10/12.

Library of Congress Cataloging-in-Publication Data

The Cataloging-in-Publication Data for *Incredible
Bugs* is on file at the Library of Congress.
ISBN 978-1-5124-0640-5 (lib. bdg.)
ISBN 978-1-5124-1166-9 (pbk.)
ISBN 978-1-5124-0922-2 (EB pdf)

Manufactured in the United States of America
1-39323-21150-3/21/2016

ANIMAL BESTS

INCREDIBLE BUGS

BY JOHN FARNDON
ILLUSTRATED BY CRISTINA PORTOLANO

HUNGRY TOMATO.

THE VOODOO WASP HAS GOT TO BE THE EERIEST TOOL—USER EVER! ITS TOOL IS NOT A STONE OR A STICK; IT'S A LIVING CATERPILLAR!

CONTENTS

SMARTEST INSECTS AND BUGS

Insects and bugs are so small that they it may be hard to believe they are clever. But some insects and bugs are very, very clever indeed. And they have special skills and characteristics that help them to survive. Prepare to be amazed!

Here's a taste of just how amazing they are, before we even move on to the really clever stuff . . .

NOISY

Cicadas (above) are super loud. They can emit a sound of 110 decibels at 20 inches (50 centimeters). Multitudes of male cicadas create the penetrating sound by vibrating membranes on their abdomens. The noise helps the cicadas drive off predators, and the sounds vary according to species.

BIG BUGS

The largest bug is the giant scarab beetle (left), which also goes by the appropriate names of elephant beetle, goliath beetle, titan beetle, and rhinoceros beetle. This giant is as big as a quarter-pound burger.

FASTEST FLIERS

It's hard to measure how fast an insect flies. But the fastest is thought to be the desert locust (above), which reaches more than 21 miles per hour (33 kilometers per hour). Corn earworm moths and deer botflies also race through the air. So do many dragonflies.

FAIRY LIGHTS

Many insects and bugs are bioluminescent. This means they glow in the dark, as do glowworms and fireflies (left). There are chemicals in the firefly's lower abdomen that shine yellow, green, or pale red. The forest can light up at twilight, as if with fairy lights, when thousands of fireflies try to attract mates or lure prey.

CLEVER!

Spiders are not insects, of course. They are arachnids which have eight legs; not six, like insects. They prey on other bugs and, like many hunters, spiders are really cunning. The Portia jumping spider is so clever it can even hunt other spiders!

I SEE YOU

A key to the Portia spider's success is its keen eyesight. Most spiders don't need to see well because they don't chase prey. They wait for prey to come to them! But the Portia's eyes see better than a cat's, so it can eye up its dangerous spider prey from a safe distance.

SECRET ATTACK

If you're a bug, the Scytodes spitting spider is deadly, spraying out a poisonous net over its victims. Yet the clever Portia manages to prey on it. It sneaks up on the spitting spider from behind, moving from cover to cover, plotting each move carefully to avoid being seen. It may even drop down on its unsuspecting victim on a thread, commando style.

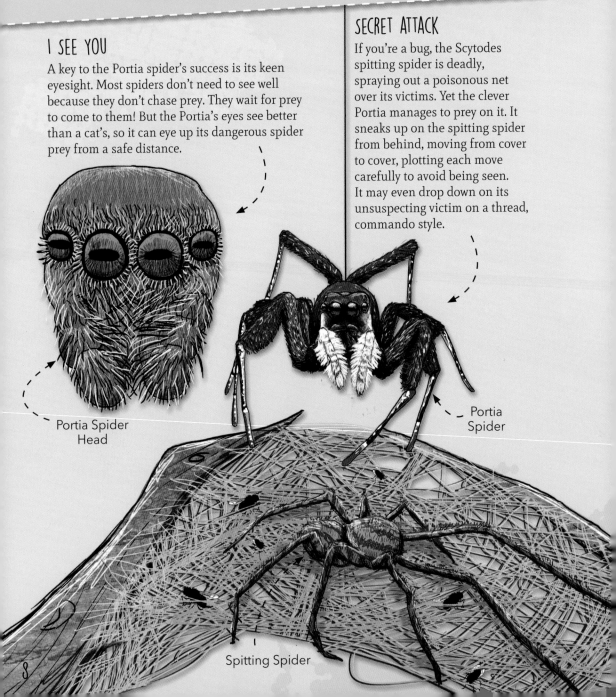

Portia Spider
Head

Portia
Spider

Spitting Spider

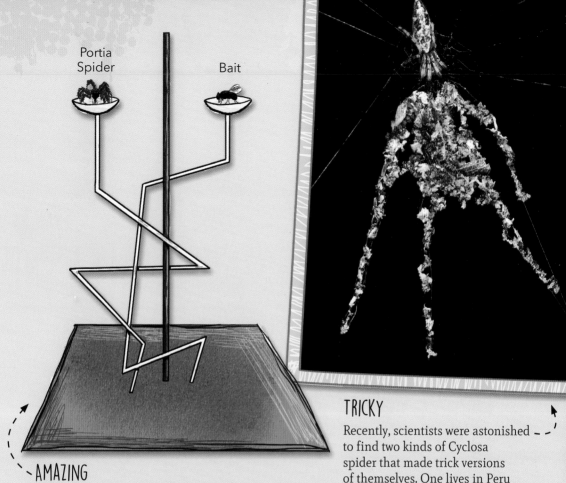

Portia
Spider

Bait

AMAZING

Scientists often test creatures' intelligence with a maze—and the Portia passes with flying colors. A hungry Portia spider is put on a platform with a view of bait. To get to the bait, the spider has to climb down, then up a maze of wires. But as it descends, it loses sight of the bait—so the spider finds the way just from its memory of where the food is. Brainy!

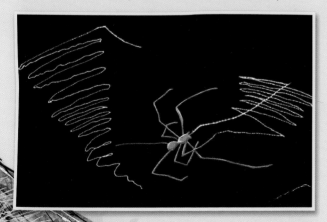

TRICKY

Recently, scientists were astonished to find two kinds of Cyclosa spider that made trick versions of themselves. One lives in Peru and the other in the Philippines. That's so far apart that scientists think there must be others living elsewhere. They seem to build giant decoy spiders from leaves and dead bugs. No one knows why. It may be to fool prey into thinking the spider's dead. Or it may be to divert the attention of predators.

SPITTING SPIDER

Most spiders weave a web and wait for victims. Not the spitting spider. It shoots out a high-speed jet of venom, silk, and glue. By waggling its fangs one thousand times a second, the jet becomes a zigzag of sticky thread that shrink-wraps its poor victim, poisoning it with venom at the same time.

GETTING THE MESSAGE

Bees are amazing. They collect pollen and nectar from flowers to make honey, and ferry pollen with them on their furry bodies. Without bees to spread pollen, most flowers and crops wouldn't grow. The most amazing of all are honeybees, which communicate in such a clever way it's almost like talking or writing.

THE LANGUAGE OF DANCE

Honeybees work together to gather nectar to turn into honey. Yet they don't know when and where flowers will bloom. So bees go out on bloom-scouting missions. The other bees can tell that a scout has found great flowers from its smell. The scout (called a worker bee) tells the others just where to find the flowers with a special dance.

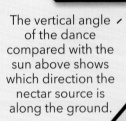

If the waggle dance is angled to the left, the nectar source is to the left.

The worker tells the other bees which direction to fly by how it dances...

If the source of nectar is close by, the worker does a simple spiral dance called a round dance. If the source of nectar is further than around 165 feet (50 meters), the bee does an amazing figure-eight dance. Bee expert Karl von Frisch named this the waggle dance.

The vertical angle of the dance compared with the sun above shows which direction the nectar source is along the ground.

The waggle dance goes up and down.

The intensity of the waggle and the number of times the bee does it tells other bees how far away the source is.

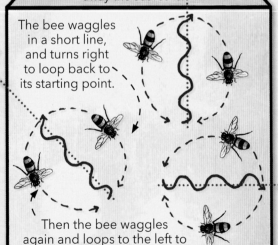

The bee waggles in a short line, and turns right to loop back to its starting point.

Then the bee waggles again and loops to the left to complete a figure-eight shape.

HONEYCOMB

The honeycomb is the remarkable nest of cells that bees make to raise their babies in, with one cell for each baby. The cells are made from beeswax and glued together with propolis, a resin from tree bark. Each cell is a hexagon, so the cells fit together perfectly. Most bees become workers. To make 1 pound (0.5 kilogram) of honey, three hundred to six hundred bees must visit two million flowers.

WHO DOES WHAT?

Honeybees are assigned different tasks to make the hive work. There is just one queen in each hive, several hundred drones, and tens of thousands of workers.

The queen lays all the eggs for new bees.

Drones are big and strong, but have no stinger and do nothing but mate with the queen.

Workers do everything else (see below).

A WORKER'S DIARY

Workers do different jobs at different times. These are the tasks they do on the different days of their short lives.

Days 1–2: Housekeeper, cleans the honeycomb cells and keeps the brood warm
Days 3–5: Nanny, feeds the older larvae with honey and pollen
Days 6–11: Nanny, feeds the younger larvae with royal jelly
Days 12–17: Builder, makes the honeycomb with wax and ripening honey
Days 18–21: Guard and air conditioner: guards the hive entrance, and pushes air in
Days 22–35: Forager: gathers pollen, nectar, propolis (tree bark resin), and water

If the waggle dance is angled to the right, the nectar source is to the right.

SPECIAL SENSES

Dragonflies may be the most perfect hunting insects ever. They have been around for at least 325 million years—long before the dinosaurs. They are probably the world's best fliers, able to fly super fast, stop in mid-air, and turn on the spot. They also have amazing eyesight and very acute senses. Very little escapes a dragonfly.

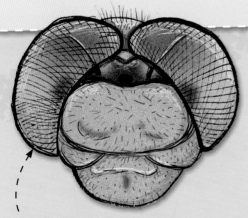

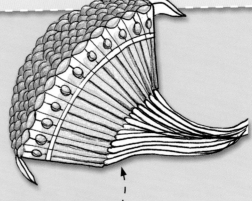

SUPER VISION

A dragonfly has compound eyes—like giant scanners with 30,000 individual cells. They are extra-sensitive to blue light, which makes the sky look really bright. So even the tiniest insect casts a dark silhouette. Although the dragonfly's eyes can't focus on distant objects, they can pick up any movement in a split second.

RAINBOW VISION

Most animals, including us, see colors as different mixes of just three colors. This is because their eyes have proteins called *opsins* that react to three colors—red, blue, and green. But the dragonfly's eyes have at least eleven kinds of opsin, so they can spot slight differences in color that would be far beyond any other animal.

ALL—SEEING

A dragonfly's giant eyes provide virtually all-round vision. They can sit still on a leaf watching, then spot prey coming from any direction and zip off after it in a split second. Their all-round vision also means dragonflies are very difficult for other predators, such as frogs, to catch.

FLIGHT INSTRUMENTS

Dragonflies are truly astonishing fliers. Using their four wings independently, they can fly fast, hover, maneuver at speed, and even fly backward and upside down. They also have a sense built into the ocelli beneath their eyes. Just like the artificial horizon in an airplane, the ocelli tells the dragonfly when it is flying level, however much it banks and turns.

COOLING OFF

Dragonflies rely on warmth for energy. But on hot days, they can overheat. So they dip their rear ends in water. The water evaporates as they fly off, keeping them super cool.

Scientists discovered that dragonflies have special neurons in their brains for tracking movement.

To avoid detection, a dragonfly attacks prey from behind and below, directly in line with its line of flight.

Dragonflies scoop up prey in their front legs.

The dragonfly predicts a flight path and adjusts its own to meet it hundreds of times every second.

CAUGHT IN MID-AIR

The dragonfly is an expert at tracking the flight of tiny insects and catching them in mid-air. It not only can spot a flying insect and decide if it's prey in 1/500th of a second; it can also track it moving at speed, too. While humans see about sixty images every second, a dragonfly sees two hundred to three hundred. To a dragonfly, a movie would look like a series of still pictures.

SUPER ATHLETES

Insects look so frail that it's easy to think they cannot be good athletes. They don't even seem to have muscles, as horses and lions do. Although insects are small, they are powerful for their size. So many insects turn out to be super athletes.

HIGH JUMP

The highest insect jump ever recorded was 28 inches (70 cm) by the froghopper. It grows less than 0.25 inches (6 millimeters) long, so that jump was way over one hundred times its length.

SPRINTERS

The fastest running insect is the Australian tiger beetle. It can reach 5.6 miles per hour (9 km/h), which is amazing considering its size. And if you allow for size, a Californian mite called *Paratarsotomus macropalpis* is even more amazing. This tiny mite can run 322 of its body lengths per second. It can even run on scorching concrete with a temperature of 140°F (60°C).

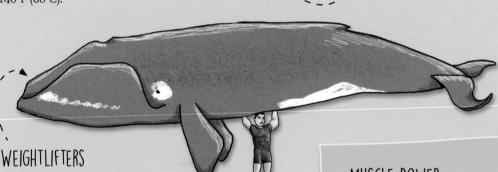

WEIGHTLIFTERS

A horned dung beetle can pull a ball of dung 1,141 times its own weight. We humans do well at pulling, too, with the aid of wheels. But the dung beetle doesn't just roll the ball—it can push it uphill. That'd be like you lifting a small whale!

MUSCLE POWER

- A froghopper can exert a force more than four hundred times its weight.
- A flea can push 135 times its weight.
- A grasshopper can exert eight times its weight.
- Humans can just about exert two to three times their weight.

ACROBATS

The acrobats of the insect world are young praying mantises. As they jump through the air, they can spin and turn entirely in control to land perfectly. They are better at this than even the world's finest gymnasts.

LONG JUMP

Fleas are long-jump champions of the bug world for their body size. They can jump two hundred times their body length! And grasshoppers are much bigger, yet still jump twenty times their body length. For a human that would be right over a tennis court lengthways and into the stands!

SPRINGTAIL

Springtails are sometimes called fleas, but they really belong to a group of tiny six-legged creatures called *hexapods*. These were among the first creatures to appear on land, nearly 400 million years ago. Springtails are super-jumpers, thanks to a spring-loaded tail called a *furcula*. This is held by a kind of catch, but when the catch is released, the bug fires into the air at rocket speed. Since neither the bug nor predators know where it will land, it's a very good escape technique!

ESCAPE ARTISTS

When you're as small as an insect or other bug, it pays to avoid being seen. You've got little hope of fighting off a hungry bird or a lizard with you on its menu. So you need to keep on the move—or keep out of sight. That's why some insects, especially the larger ones that make tasty meals, are very good at disguise and camouflage.

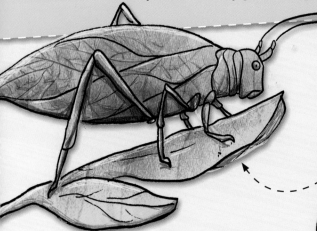

KATYDIDN'T

Perhaps the masters of insect camouflage are katydids. They are colored green with little spots of brown just like the leaves they live among. They are even shaped like leaves, and have the same veined pattern. When they're resting during the day, they are very hard to spot indeed.

I'M AN OWL!

Owls are formidable and dangerous hunters for any small creature. So if you're a butterfly, what better way to put off hunting birds than by convincing them you're an owl. That's what owl butterflies in tropical Latin America do. They're big butterflies, and their wings are colored to look like an owl's face, with dark spots that look just like an owl's big eyes.

MOTH OR LEAF?

Moths tend to fly at night when there is less danger around. That means they have to rest during the day. But resting in broad daylight could be lethal. That's why, unlike butterflies, they usually have drab colors. In fact, they tend to adopt the colors of the places where they settle. That's why some moths are colored to look like tree bark. The poplar hawk moth isn't just colored like a dead leaf; the edges of its wings are crinkled like one, too.

STICK INSECTS

Some insects' wings are shaped and colored to look like leaves. Stick insects' entire bodies are shaped to look just like old twigs. Some stick insects are very beautifully colored; others are very drab. But they are all very long and thin. In fact, looking like a twig means that they can grow very long indeed. The longest is Chan's stick insect, *Phobaeticus chani*, at 23 inches (58 cm), making it one of the world's biggest insects.

I'M A SNAKE!

Few predators are brave enough to attack a poisonous snake. Yet a plump and slow caterpillar looks like a ready meal. The sphinx moth caterpillar has a clever solution to this problem. It has a couple of spots on its body that look just like a snake's eyes.

I'M A FLOWER!

The Orchid Mantis preys on insects that feed on orchid flowers. So it's evolved to be shaped and colored just like an orchid. When insects come to feed on what they think is a flower, they find themselves in the clutches of the mantis. What's more, the mantis has made itself so colorful and pretty that some insects choose to try out the mantis rather than a safe and real flower nearby.

BRILLIANT BUILDERS

Some insects, such as bees, wasps, and ants, live together in colonies. By working together, millions of insects, such as termites, can create a giant nest. Each termite has its own job to do. Smaller worker termites gather food, dig tunnels, and care for the young. Larger soldier termites defend the colony from attack and build the nest. The result of this teamwork is an astonishing termite city.

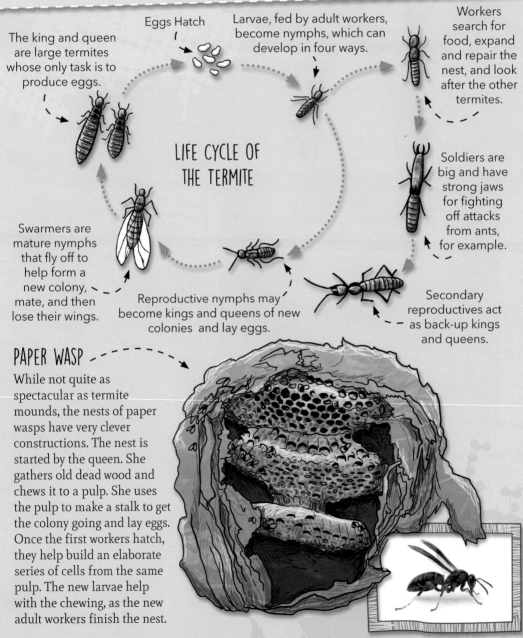

LIFE CYCLE OF THE TERMITE

The king and queen are large termites whose only task is to produce eggs.

Eggs Hatch

Larvae, fed by adult workers, become nymphs, which can develop in four ways.

Workers search for food, expand and repair the nest, and look after the other termites.

Soldiers are big and have strong jaws for fighting off attacks from ants, for example.

Secondary reproductives act as back-up kings and queens.

Reproductive nymphs may become kings and queens of new colonies and lay eggs.

Swarmers are mature nymphs that fly off to help form a new colony, mate, and then lose their wings.

PAPER WASP

While not quite as spectacular as termite mounds, the nests of paper wasps have very clever constructions. The nest is started by the queen. She gathers old dead wood and chews it to a pulp. She uses the pulp to make a stalk to get the colony going and lay eggs. Once the first workers hatch, they help build an elaborate series of cells from the same pulp. The new larvae help with the chewing, as the new adult workers finish the nest.

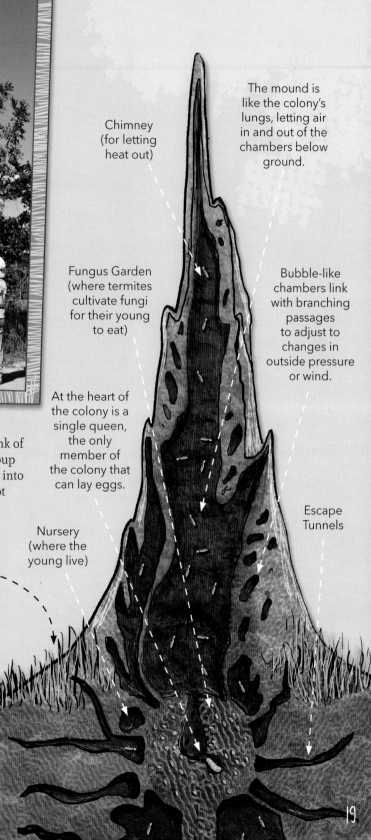

Chimney
(for letting
heat out)

The mound is
like the colony's
lungs, letting air
in and out of the
chambers below
ground.

Fungus Garden
(where termites
cultivate fungi
for their young
to eat)

Bubble-like
chambers link
with branching
passages
to adjust to
changes in
outside pressure
or wind.

At the heart of
the colony is a
single queen,
the only
member of
the colony that
can lay eggs.

Escape
Tunnels

Nursery
(where the
young live)

LIFE ROLES

Scientists are beginning to think of termite colonies as a single group brain. The termites aren't born into their different roles. They adopt them when needed, guided by chemicals called *pheromones*.

MOUND CITY

Mound-building termites live in Africa, Australia, and South America. A mound termite is smaller than a pumpkin seed. But a whole termite colony can build nest mounds more than 17 feet (5 m) high. To do this, the colony moves more than a quarter of a ton of soil, and a lot more water. Inside, the termite mound is like a little city, with tunnels and chambers. It even has a ventilation system.

19

WEBMAKERS

The webs that spiders make to catch prey are some of the most remarkable of all natural structures. They are created with silk threads that ooze from a spider's spinneret glands. Different glands make different threads for particular purposes. Spider silk is one of the strongest natural materials on Earth—six times as strong for its weight as the best steel.

ORB WEB

The most familiar spiderweb is the orb web. It's easily seen as a big wheel shape stretched out between branches. It often catches dew in the night and sparkles in the morning sun. But this beauty is a trap. The threads are sticky and hard to see. An insect can easily fly into the web and become stuck. As the insect struggles, the spider detects the vibrations and moves in to claim its dinner—often paralyzing it with venom and wrapping it up in silk to eat later.

SPINNING A WEB

All webs start with a single thread of silk. With an orb web, the spider lets this thread drift in the wind until it sticks to another branch to make a bridge. The spider crawls over the thread and releases another to form a V. Then it lowers itself from this to create a Y-shape (1). It ties this off with more anchor lines to set out the basic support for the web (2). The spider then moves around in ever-widening spirals from the center to complete the web (3, 4).

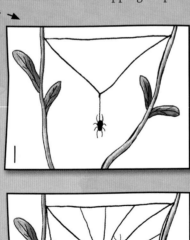

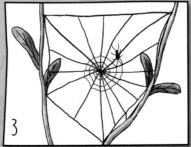

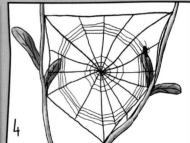

KINDS OF WEBS

Besides the familiar orb, there are many other kinds of webs. Here are some of the most common ones, with the scientific name of the spider or spider group that makes them. Not all spiders use their webs to catch their prey. Trapdoor spiders hide behind webs and then pounce. Net-casting spiders throw their webs over victims.

Orb Web
(*Araneidae* family)

Orb Web
(*Tetragnathidae* family)

Cribellate Orb Web
(*Uloboridae* family)

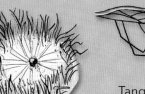

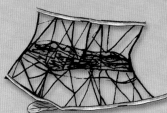

Funnel Web
(*Agelenopsis* family)

Tangle Web of
Black Widow
(*Theridiidae* family)

Sheet Web
(*Frontinella* family)

Female Argiope Spider
(wrapping up a grasshopper
caught in the web)

Tangle Web
(*Steatoda* family)

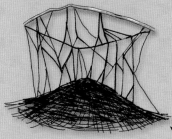

Web of Labyrinth Spider,
(*Metepeira labyrinthea*)

Web of Basilica Orbweaver,
(*Mecynogea lemniscata*)

TEAMWORK

Perhaps the greatest team players in the world are ants. They are really tiny, and individually they are not very clever. But by working together in every way, they achieve amazing things. They have no leader and no plan, yet together they perform difficult tasks and build complex structures.

TAKING A LEAF

Leafcutter ants are farmers, growing their own food in underground fungus farms. Each ant carries a piece of leaf up to fifty times its body weight back to the colony, in a giant procession. The leaves are used to create fungus gardens that feed the entire colony.

ANTS ON THE MARCH

Army ants are so-named because when there is a food shortage, the whole colony moves out like an army. They form a giant column, millions of insects strong, crawling over the ground. The ants fiercely defend themselves against anything in their way. A wounded or immobilized animal may be quickly devoured. The jaws of the African army ant (below) are so powerful that tribespeople use them as emergency stitches on a wound.

AFRICAN ARMY ANTS

Soldier

Minor Worker

Worker

ANT BRIDGE

One of the most extraordinary structures that ants create is a bridge. When they need to cross between two distant branches, a team makes a bridge with their bodies for the others to cross. The strength that the ants need to build out into mid-air, and then hold on while other ants walk across them is astonishing. Scientists are only just beginning to learn how ants act together to perform feats like this. They think that the ants are responding to simple signals that build together to create a complex pattern.

LEAFCUTTER CITY

Leafcutter ants build the closest thing to human cities in the natural world. Their giant structures can be 250 feet (80 m) across and provide a home for 8 million ants or more. It takes several years to build this complex city, with separate tunnels and chambers for farming leaves, breeding, raising young, and more.

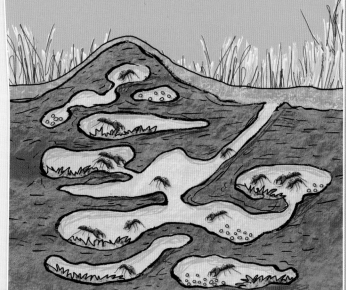

LIFE RAFT

When their home is flooded, all ants in a colony gather together to form a huge raft. They float on the water until its level goes down and they can find a new home. It is thought that the raft-building depends on the way the outside members shape themselves, so that new members are encouraged to join on and extend the raft.

TOOL USERS

Because humans use tools, it seems that this is a real test of an animal's intelligence. There are very few insects that use tools. But that may be because they have no need to—and because they are mostly very small. However, the hunting wasp seems to use a tool. And other wasps use a living "tool" to protect their young.

VOODOO WASP

The voodoo wasp (top right) has got to be the eeriest tool-user ever! Its tool is not a stone or a stick—it's a living caterpillar, which it uses like a tool. The wasp lays its eggs inside caterpillars of the geometrid moth.

The voodoo wasp lays its eggs in the caterpillar.

After the eggs hatch, the larvae feed on the caterpillar's body fluid, and then eat their way out to spin their cocoons on a nearby branch.

Wasp Pupae

Now the caterpillar becomes a zombie. It forms a protective arch over the cocoons, without moving or feeding. It thrashes wildly if another insect approaches. Once the adult wasps finally emerge from their cocoons, the zombie caterpillar drops dead.

STONE AGE

The hunting wasp is a solitary wasp that makes its nest in a burrow in sandy soil. It stocks up the burrow with a paralyzed caterpillar and throws it in sand to seal the entrance. Then, remarkably, it picks up a stone in its mandibles and uses it as a tool to pat down the sand into place.

CAN YOU TAKE IT?

The sting of the tarantula hawk wasp is sheer agony —but the sting of a bullet ant is worse. Yet boys of the Satere-Mawe tribe in the Brazilian rain forest need to prove they are men. So they put their hand inside a glove packed with hundreds of bullet ants for ten minutes. The sting paralyzes their arm and leaves them shaking uncontrollably for days. They go through this ritual twenty times to prove themselves.

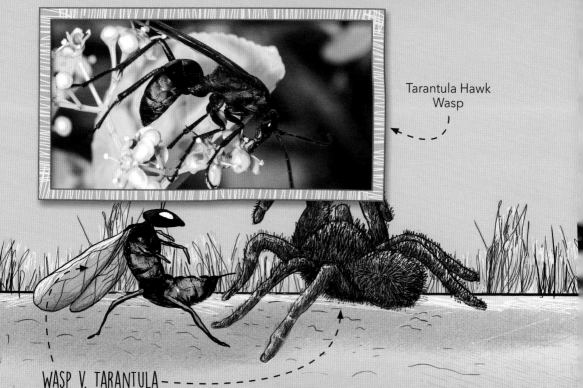

Tarantula Hawk Wasp

WASP V. TARANTULA

Surely one of the deadliest fights in the bug world must be between the tarantula hawk wasp and the tarantula spider. But it's the wasp that wins. It paralyzes the tarantula with a sting so fierce that humans scream in agony if they're stung. It then drags the spider into its den, and lays an egg. The egg hatches into a larva, which over several weeks devours the paralyzed tarantula alive!

JOURNEY INSECTS

Butterflies may seem to drift where the wind takes them. But the monarch butterfly is one of the natural world's great navigators. It can migrate huge distances. Some moths and dragonflies make great journeys, too.

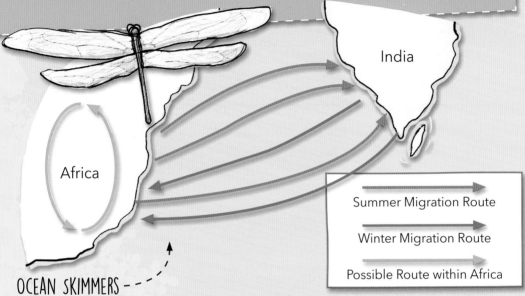

India

Africa

Summer Migration Route

Winter Migration Route

Possible Route within Africa

OCEAN SKIMMERS

The greatest insect migrators are golden skimmer dragonflies. They make an annual round trip of more than 11,000 miles (17,700 km)—and most of that nonstop flight is not over land, but over open ocean. Late in the year, they head southwest from India, flying very high to avoid headwinds. Apparently stopping only briefly at the Maldive and Seychelles Islands, they fly right over the Indian Ocean to Africa. The following April they return to India.

BUGONG GONE

The bugong moth of Australia migrates huge distances. They try to escape summer heat, rather than winter cold. In spring, they fly 600 miles (1,000 km) south from the plains of Queensland and western New South Wales to spend the summer in the cool caves of the Australian Alps. Some caves are carpeted 5 feet (1.5 m) thick with dead moth bodies, built up over thousands of generations.

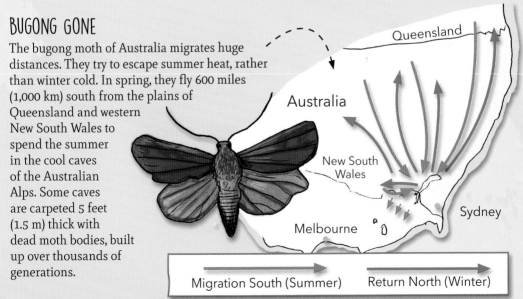

Queensland

Australia

New South Wales

Melbourne

Sydney

Migration South (Summer)   Return North (Winter)

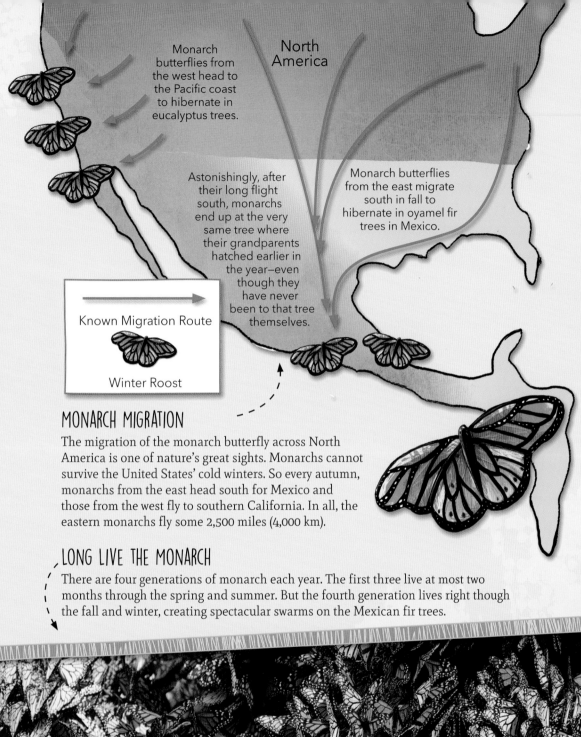

Monarch butterflies from the west head to the Pacific coast to hibernate in eucalyptus trees.

North America

Astonishingly, after their long flight south, monarchs end up at the very same tree where their grandparents hatched earlier in the year—even though they have never been to that tree themselves.

Monarch butterflies from the east migrate south in fall to hibernate in oyamel fir trees in Mexico.

→ Known Migration Route

Winter Roost

MONARCH MIGRATION

The migration of the monarch butterfly across North America is one of nature's great sights. Monarchs cannot survive the United States' cold winters. So every autumn, monarchs from the east head south for Mexico and those from the west fly to southern California. In all, the eastern monarchs fly some 2,500 miles (4,000 km).

LONG LIVE THE MONARCH

There are four generations of monarch each year. The first three live at most two months through the spring and summer. But the fourth generation lives right though the fall and winter, creating spectacular swarms on the Mexican fir trees.

THE BEST OF THE BEST

JUMPING SPIDERS
SPECIES: 5,000
LIVE IN: Most places, especially tropical forests
EAT: Mostly other spiders and insects

Jumping spiders are the ninjas of the spider world. Rather than spinning a web and waiting for prey, they sneak up on it and pounce.

BEES
SPECIES: 20,000
LIVE IN: Any place that has flowers
EAT: Flower nectar and pollen

Bees are the main way that flowers spread their pollen. Honeybees make honey.

DRAGONFLIES
SPECIES: 3,000
LIVE IN: Everywhere on land, except very cold places
EAT: Mostly mosquitoes, flies, and small wasps

Dragonflies are closely related to damselflies, but it is dragonflies that are the insect world's master fliers. Many have brilliant shimmering colors

FLEAS
SPECIES: More than 2,000
LIVE IN: On animals almost everywhere
EAT: The blood of mammals and birds

Fleas are tiny wingless insects that move by jumping. They live as parasites, eating the blood of host animals, such as cats, dogs, and rats.

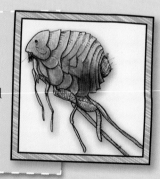

MOTHS
SPECIES: 160,000
LIVE IN: Most places where plants grow
EAT: Flower nectar and the juice of rotting fruit

Moths have large wings and hairy bodies. They mostly fly at night and rest during the day, unlike butterflies, which fly mostly in the day.

TERMITES

SPECIES: 3,100
LIVE IN: Everywhere on land but Antarctica—especially Africa, South America, and Asia
EAT: Rotting plant matter and soft timber

These mostly flightless insects live in giant colonies where tasks are divided between vast numbers of workers and drones, and a few kings and queens.

SPIDERS

SPECIES: 45,700
LIVE IN: Everywhere on land except Antarctica
EAT: Mostly small insects

Unlike insects, which have six legs, spiders have eight, and can't fly. Most can spin silk threads for weaving into webs to catch prey.

ANTS

SPECIES: 22,000
LIVE IN: Everywhere on land but Antarctica
EAT: Mostly bugs, but some feed on fungus

Most ants form large colonies. The biggest ant colonies are the most complex structures built by animals, apart from humans.

WASPS

SPECIES: At least 100,000
LIVE IN: Everywhere on land except Antarctica
EAT: Insects, nectar, tree sap, and fruit

Wasps are related to bees. But unlike bees, they are predators and mostly solitary. They have a nastier sting than bees.

BUTTERFLIES

SPECIES: 18,500
LIVE IN: Everywhere on land where there are flowers
EAT: Caterpillars eat leaves; adults eat flower nectar

Butterflies change dramatically from their young larval stage as creepy-crawly caterpillars to large colorful winged adults, in a process known as metamorphosis.

SPECIAL SKILLS

There are many insects and bugs that have a skill that's so special and so much more amazing than anything humans could do. With so many insects and bugs in the world, the range of skills is wide.

THE ULTIMATE SURVIVORS

Most people scream when they see a cockroach. But that probably doesn't bother cockroaches. They are the ultimate survivors. Their brains contain antibiotics that fight off deadly diseases, such as MRSA, better than any drugs we have. Cockroaches can also survive nuclear explosions. When atomic bombs were dropped on Hiroshima and Nagasaki in Japan in 1945, cockroaches were the only living things to survive unscathed.

PRIMED TO ESCAPE

Cicadas have an escape tactic worthy of a master criminal. They spend many years of the early part of their life buried underground, emerging only briefly as adults to breed. Amazingly, all the millions of cicadas in one area emerge at exactly the same time. No one knows how they manage this feat of timing. But it means there are far too many of them for predators to eat. What's more, they only emerge after thirteen or seventeen years. These are numbers that cannot be divided. This means that no predator could evolve a regular cycle that would catch the cicadas when they emerge.

SONIC JAMMERS

It's well-known that bats find things in the dark by emitting high-pitch sounds. What's less known is that the tiger moth, which might be dinner for a bat, can detect these sounds, so it knows when bats are coming. What's more, the tiger moth can even jam the bat's sonar signal and confuse it. Using fake sonic images, the moth can make bats "see" things that aren't there. For the bat, this is like being surrounded by camera flashes popping up all over the place in a pitch dark room.

AQUA SPIDER

Fishing spiders get their name because they can actually catch small fish! They run across the water as if it was dry land, then plunge their sharp front legs into the water to catch the fish by surprise. Then they inject it with venom from their jaws and haul it back to shore. The spider can also climb right under the water for forty-five minutes, breathing air trapped in its hairs.

SUPER WEAPONS

The bombardier beetle has a devastating secret weapon that earned it its name. It's basically a chemical gun on legs. When threatened, the bombardier can fire out a jet of boiling hot liquid. And that liquid is not just super-hot, but also a highly toxic mix of hydrogen peroxide and hydroquinone. When those two chemicals mix, the result is explosive. So the beetle stores each in separate glands at the end of its abdomen, and mixes them only when it fires its jet in anger.

INDEX

THE AUTHOR

John Farndon is Royal Literary Fellow at Anglia Ruskin University in Cambridge, United Kingdom, and the author of a huge number of books for adults and children on science, technology, and nature, including international best-sellers. He has been shortlisted four times for the Royal Society's Young People's Book Prize.

THE ILLUSTRATOR

Cristina Portolano was born in Naples, Italy, and studied in Bologna and Paris, graduating in Comics and Illustration. Her artwork has appeared in Italian magazines and comic books such as *Delebile* and *Teiera*. She lives and works in Bologna, and her first book has recently been published by Topipittori.